Dan Locklair

RUBRICS

*a liturgical suite for organ
in five movements*

e.c. kerby ltd.

DISTRIBUTED BY

HAL•LEONARD®
CORPORATION

7777 W. BLUEMOUND RD. P.O. BOX 13819 MILWAUKEE, WI 53213

RUBRICS

(A Liturgical Suite for Organ in Five Movements)
by
Dan Locklair

RUBRICS was composed during the Spring of 1988 in Winston-Salem, North Carolina on a commission from the Organ Artists Series of Pittsburgh, Pennsylvania for their tenth anniversary year celebration (culminating on April 16, 1989 with the World Premiere of RUBRICS in Pittsburgh by the American organist, Mary Preston).

RUBRICS may be performed as a five-movement suite or its movements may be played separately. The extra-musical impetus and subsequent titles for each movement of RUBRICS are found in the instructions (rubrics) to the services for THE BOOK OF COMMON PRAYER (September, 1979). The source for each movement, along with a brief program note, is given below.

1. ["The ancient praise-shout,] 'Hallelujah,' has been restored. . ." (The Psalter, page 584)
    This energetic, dialoguing movement is based on the pitches, F, G, C, D.

2. "Silence may be kept." (Daily Morning Prayer : Rite One, page 41)
    This lyrical movement, featuring the flute stops of the organ, is in the Lydian mode and is centered on "F."

3. ". . .and thanksgivings may follow." (Daily Morning Prayer : Rite One, page 58)
    This dance-like trumpet tune in trio style (with intermittent recitative-like sections) primarily uses the pitches, A, B, C-sharp, E, F-sharp for its musical material.

4. "The Peace may be exchanged." (Thanksgiving for . . . a Child, page 445)
    This lyrical aria, featuring a solo diapason color (accompanied by strings and double pedal throughout), is based in D Major.

5. "The people respond - Amen!" (An Order for Celebrating the Holy Eucharist, page 401)
    An energetic toccata, this finale is primarily based on the transposition of the four pitches that make up Movement 1, E-flat, F, A-flat, B-flat. With the addition of these four pitches to those of the primary pitch material of Movements 1 and 3, all twelve pitches of the chromatic scale are now fully represented.

*****

Notes to the performer:

Registrations are only suggestions and may be freely adapted to any instrument. Suggestions are given for a 4-manual organ, but the piece can easily be adapted to a 2 or 3-manual organ.
Manual indications are as follows:

I	Choir
II	Great
III	Swell
IV	Solo or Bombarde

Organ chimes are called for in Movement 2 and a Zymblestern in Movement 3. These stops are optional, though their use, when available, will enhance the respective movements.

Timings:

1.	ca. 2'
2.	ca. 2' 30"
3.	ca. 2' 30"
4.	ca. 2' 20"
5.	ca. 2'

ca. 11' 20" total duration

Dan Locklair
May 1988
Winston-Salem, North Carolina

RUBRICS
A Liturgical Suite for Organ

1. " . . . 'Hallelujah,' has been restored . . ."

Dan Locklair

Registration:
Foundations, mixtures and reeds on manuals and pedal. All coupled.

[May use antiphonal division (if available) in pedal.]

2. "Silence may be kept."

Registration:
I: Flutes. 8', 4' (equal to III)
II*: Flutes. 8', 4'
(slightly more prominent than I or III)
III*: Flutes. 8',4'
(equal to I)
Pedal: Flute 8'

Manuals

[* use for 2 - manual organ]

Pedal

Reflective and never hurried (𝅗𝅥 = ca. 46)

Very flexible and expressive (𝅗𝅥 = ca. 92 [or 𝅝 = ca. 46])   Slowing _ _ _ _ _ _ _

+ 𝄀 = free meter with ♩ getting the beat.

* The R.H. color may be more prominent (especially on a 2-manual organ).
  It is always important that the second color be an obvious, blending after-effect to the first color.

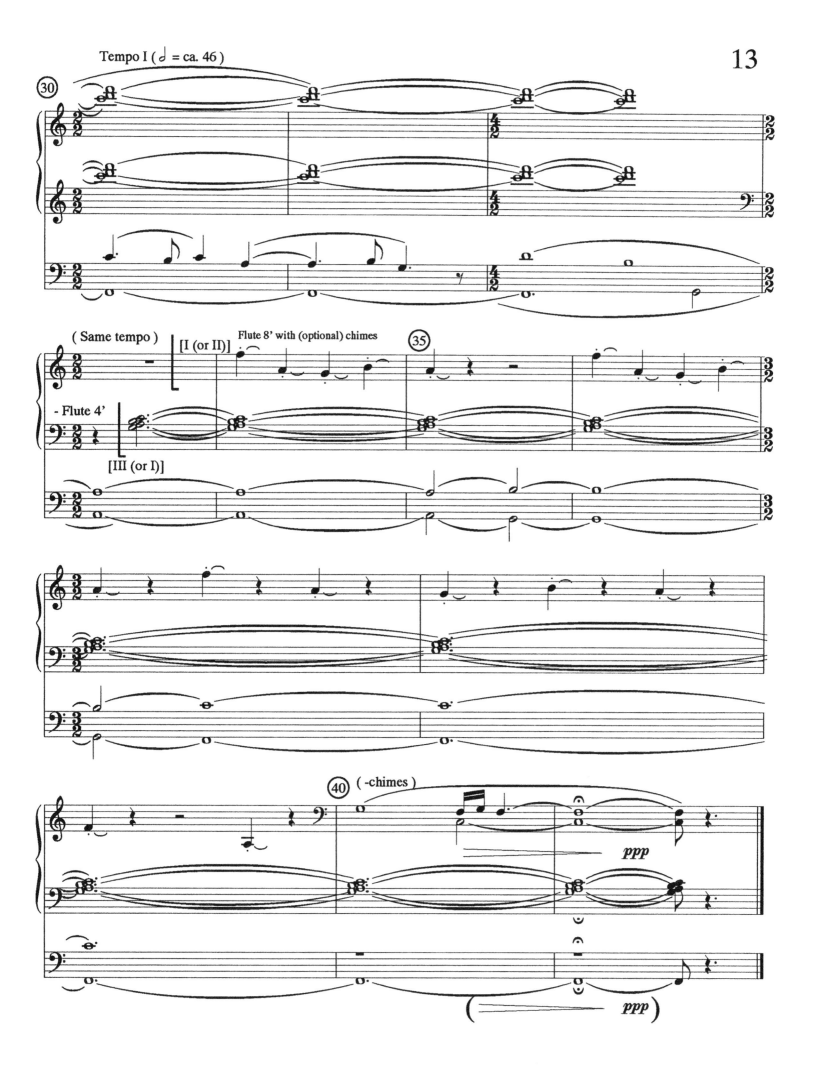

Registration:

III or (I): Sprightly foundations and mixtures
IV (or II): Trumpet 8'
Pedal: Light 16', 8'
(III or I to pedal)

Quick and dance-like
(♩ = ca. 144)

Freely shaped in free tempo (Tempo II)

Tempo I (♩ = ca. 144) [+ zymb.]

* **0** = free meter

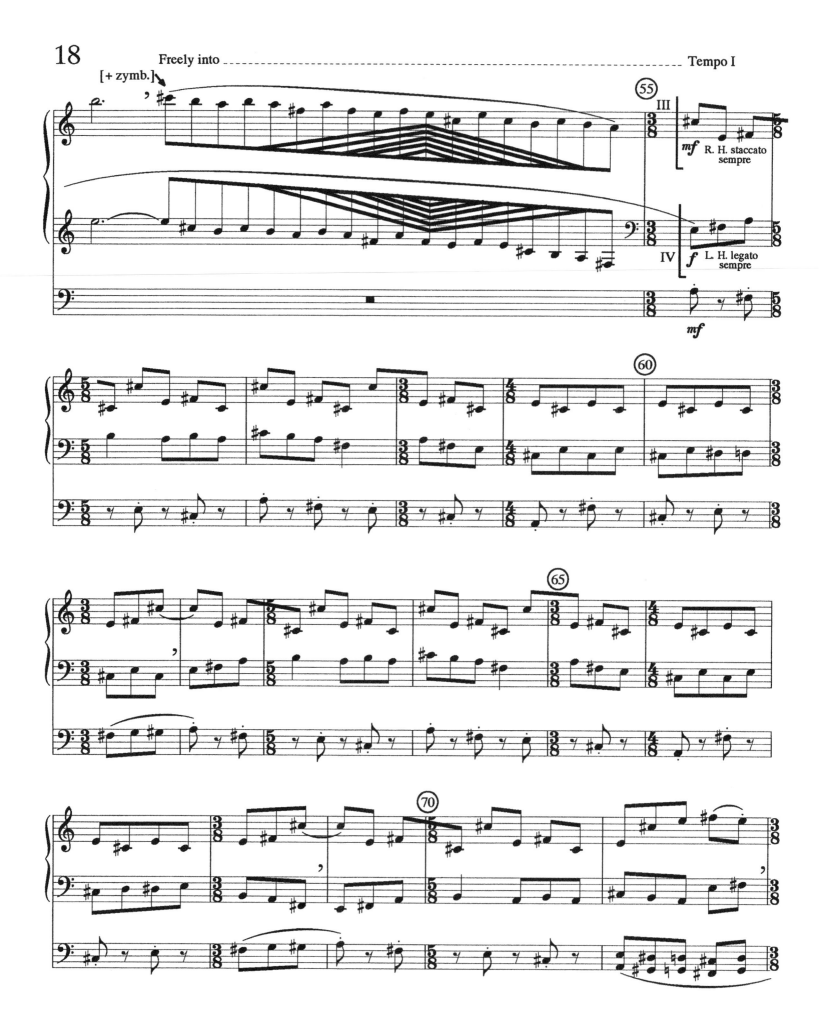

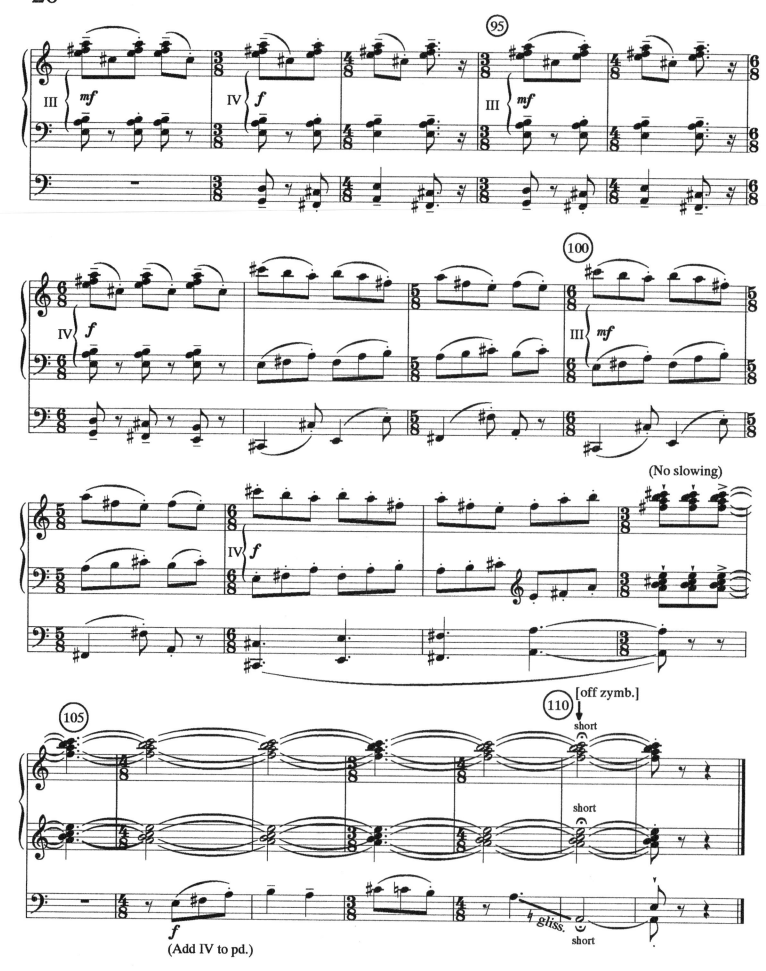

4. "The Peace may be exchanged."

Registration:

II: Diapason 8'
(optional tremolo)
III (or I): Celeste
strings 8'
Pedal: III (or I)
to pedal

5. "The people respond - Amen!"

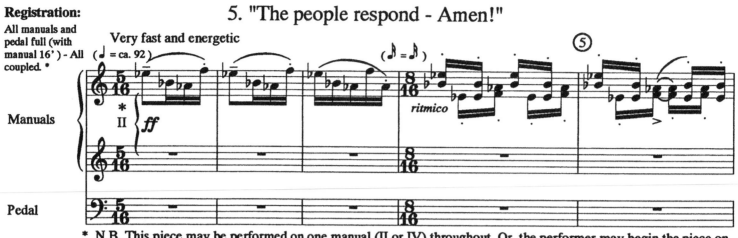

* N.B. This piece may be performed on one manual (II or IV) throughout. Or, the performer may begin the piece on I or III, move to II at ㉘, move to IV (and /or add) at ㉖, and add at ⑦⑥ and ⑧⑧. Adjust pedal accordingly.

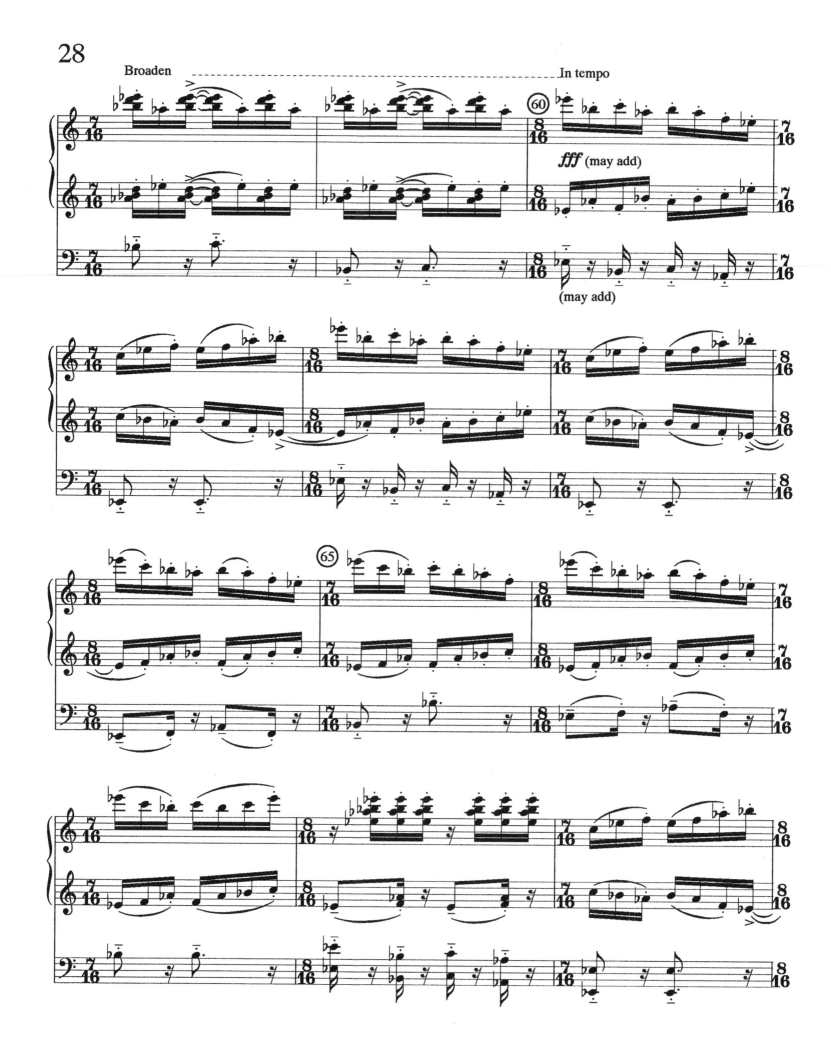

Winston-Salem, N.C.
May 1988